# TWICE AS GOOD

## In Half The Time

I0555043

## Adrian J.R. Davis

TrueVinePublishing.org

Twice as Good in Half the Time
Adrian J. R. Davis

Published by
True Vine Publishing Co
810 Dominican Dr. Ste 103
Nashville, TN 37228
www.TrueVinePublishing.org

ISBN: 978-1-956469-72-1 Paperback
ISBN: 978-1-956469-73-8 eBook

Printed in the United States—First Printing

# Table of Contents

This book is dedicated to those who are on a quest for self-development and hungry to find out who you are and what journey you are on.

# Defining Good

The definition of "Good" is *to be desired or approved of.* Another definition states "Good" is *a benefit or advantage to someone or something.* I gravitate to the second definition of "good." I believe that we are all here to be a benefit or an advantage to people.

When people ask me about becoming valuable, I admonish them to see who they were valuable to. If they don't know at that time, I advise them to think from the perspective of who they want to be valuable to.

This is a shift in thought. Most people are only reacting to what is in their face at the moment, not knowing that what is "now" is a derivative of what has happened in the past-- your past decision, your past reactions, and your past thoughts.

So to question who you are valuable to now is not as important as who you would like to be valuable to in the future. You can take this mentality into many areas in your life - Work, family, and community.

Let's look at this concept from a business perspective. Think of some of the brands that stand out to you and may be in your household right now. How did they get there? I know you went out and bought them or ordered them, but think a little deeper. How did they end up in your house?

Apparently, you found value in the product and decided to give it a try. If you liked it, you kept coming back for more. In some cases, because of the brand, you may have multiple products from the same brand  because you trusted them for one product and decided to extend purchasing power to get another product.

Let's think about the Johnson and Johnson brand. They don't just create one product. Many people who use a Johnson and Johnson product don't just use one of their products, they use multiple ones in their line-up. If they trusted this company to be their go to for skin-care needs, then they are more open to allowing their products to be a self-care provider as well.

The same thing happens with us. We are a brand and we must know that some person or organization really needs or wants what we are offering; and if we get "Good" at what we provide, we have opportunities to provide more services for longer periods of time.

So defining what good looks like is important for you just like it is for corporations. They do extensive research to figure out what type of person is using their product(s) and why. Once they have a firm understanding of their market, they market to that area in their life. You can do the exact same thing.

First, understanding what you do well is paramount. If you are technical in nature and love that space and have been given praise for your work consistently, you may want to focus in on this. An indicator of your gift is that people around you find your work difficult, but you find it to be super easy. An indicator of value transfer and that you may be good is when people are in awe of the work you do.

## Be Good for the Right People

The other element to work from is knowing that being good at something means nothing if it is not in front of the right people.

I will keep it light-hearted here. If you love action movies and despise romantic comedies, then it will not matter how beautifully written and directed that movie is. You won't like it. I can share how the characters fall in love and how the on-screen presence works so well with each other, but that will not move the needle for you.

The same exists for you. If you are amazing, but what you do is not a fit for the people you are in front of, then it will simply not work.

This brings up another very important point: you can compare yourself only to yourself in this journey.

# Notes

_____

_____

_____

_____

_____

_____

_____

_____

_____

_____

_____

_____

_____

_____

_____

_____

_____

_____

# Compare You to You

If you see someone doing well in another industry and you try to take your strengths and abilities to that industry to have the same success, you could fail, especially if your skills are related to another industry or area. There are great bakers in this world and they would do well to know their skills and know who wants what they are creating. However, if for some reason they seek to look at a chef and say, "Wow, I believe I could do that with my baking skills", there could be some misalignment of expectations.

This is where many people lose their will to go on; comparing themselves to others. Your journey is your journey and what you have to offer should only be compared to how you can do it and with what energy you can bring to it.

There are many public speakers. But, the

thing that makes a speaker really good and allows him or her to stand out from others is being original--being themselves!

I don't want to confuse the notion that you can't learn from others. But there is a BIG difference in learning from others and wanting to adopt their blueprint as your own. Doing the latter will drain you more and leave you wanting to recalibrate.

The great Tony Robbins has made a name for himself as a motivational speaker and personal development coach. Robbins' mentor was Jim Rohn. Jim Rohn was amazing in his own right. His style was much more laid back and comical, whereas Tony Robbins' approach is more "in-your-face" and boisterous. Notice, that I said that Jim Rohn was Tony's mentor. However, Tony did not gain his fame being just like his mentor, he gained it being himself.

Now millions of people and hundreds of countries later, Tony Robbins is someone's mentor and hopefully that person is looking to see what works for them.

The individualization and authenticity of you is what people are drawn to when you offer a service or a product. This is why knowing what you are good at and discovering how you want to present it to the world is paramount in being your best version of good.

When I spoke earlier about how some brands are in your home and why that may be, it was because of their originality and their impression on you. There are some things that people will swear by and will not deviate from them. The brand has built brand power with the constituent. If they were like everyone else, there would be no need for people to build an attachment. They could just use any brand.

When you are only comparing yourself to yourself and becoming the best for the people you intend to serve or provide products to, then by default you create a following that will identify with you.

I remember working in learning and development early on in my career. I felt that the content was stuffy and that it lacked the life needed to be fun. See, I believe that in order for people to really have a good learning experience, they first must want to be in that learning environment. I quickly realized that the people who were facilitating many of these classes were only doing it as a job and that they had not tried to give a little bit of their personality to the training.

When I got the opportunity to do my first classes, I remember saying to myself people have to laugh and enjoy themselves. I will make sure that happens.

Years later, many companies call for me to come into their organizations to do leadership development, not because I have created the most profound training design ever created, but because I get people to respond. In my line of work, that is what really counts-- having people to change their behaviors. My methods are the vehicle that will get people to the destination of change, and that works for the executives that are looking for that result.

I will say, that when I tried to copy a blueprint that was already out there, it did not fit my life; it only left me scratching my head and wondering where I went wrong?

Be you, but be really good at it!

# Notes

_____

_____

_____

_____

_____

_____

_____

_____

_____

_____

_____

_____

_____

_____

_____

_____

_____

_____

# Your Current Location

**E**ver walked into a mall or arrived at a theme park? There is usually a board that has in big writing, "You Are Here".

This applies in life. Many of us don't really know where we are. That can be frustrating when you believe you know where you want to go, but not sure how long it is going to take you or what direction is best for you to move towards.

This is how this sounds in real life: I want to become a millionaire, I would like to buy a new house, I want to be the next VP of this department, etc. These are lofty goals, but having these in the distance and not having a plan for how to get there will cause frustration and loss of time, and could lead to loss of motivation.

I remember I was taking my son to get some new basketball shoes. We walked into the mall from a side door, I had a general idea of where I wanted to go. In fact, we even saw the logo from the outside of the mall. But this mall was massive and there were so many ways we could go to hopefully get where we were intending to go. After walking for a few minutes, I stepped over to the side and said, "we need to find one of those mall maps."

Once we got to the nearest map we realized that when we came in we took a right and started walking down the hallway. The store was much closer to us if we would have taken a left when we came into the doors.

Nevertheless, neither my son nor I felt depressed, probably to the contrary. We knew where we were in reference to the shoe store that we needed to visit.

When you look at that map in the mall or at the theme park, what emotions are emitted from you knowing you now have a plan to get to where you want to go?

If you truly asked yourself this question and thought about those emotions, think about how much more impactful it is when you figure out where you are in life in reference to where you want to go.

If you really want to know where you currently are, you will need to be honest with yourself and be okay with some objective feedback. It may be humbling, but it will start you on the path that you want to be, with clearer bearings, than if you were aimlessly walking around believing you were at one place in your life and really not there.

I remember I wanted to be an international speaker and trainer. I had an opportunity to work with a massive organization. I am talking about 470,000- employees-or-more type of massive. When I got a call to come in and interview with them, they asked me to share a snippet of a training so that they could see my skills.

I was excited about the opportunity and, frankly, was a little overconfident too. I went in and started to share my training. The panel got a chance to see my facilitation style and I thought I had knocked it out of the park.

My subject for that day was on the Generations in the Workplace. I was confident that I had provided all the nuggets I should to impress the panel. To my delight, it looked as though they were eating my presentation up. I was a success! I was definitely about to have an opportunity to work with this giant organization.

As we wrapped up the interviewing session, and the hiring manager was walking me out of the building, he kindly let me know that my presentation was good. He also provided a statement to me about latch-key kids in Japan and India. He said, "I bet the time line for latch-key kids in Japan and India are probably different from the US. Their cultural development doesn't mirror ours years for years. You did well, we hope to be talking to you soon."

At that moment, I realized that my starting point was U.S. based knowledge at best and I really needed to skill up on my international cultural studies if I was going to be doing international work and talking to international teams.

Just like that story of my goal to speak and train internationally, many of you have goals that are lofty and ambitious. There is nothing wrong with that. In fact it should be applauded. However, for you to get off to the best start, you must start with the reality of where you are currently and then develop a plan to move from there.

# Notes

_____

_____

_____

_____

_____

_____

_____

_____

_____

_____

_____

_____

_____

_____

_____

_____

_____

_____

_____

# How Far Do You Have To Go?

This moves me into the next point which is determining how far you have to go.

Have you ever been on a road trip with kids? You ever hear the repeated question: "are we there yet?" It can sometimes get down right annoying when you have heard it for the 500th time in the last two hours. You want to find the all illusive human mute button, but there hasn't been one created. I digress! The reason you hear this soul throbbing question multiple times during a road trip is that there is no correct time expectation.

In a kid's mind, they believe that it is going to

be fun to travel from Florida to California by car. Then, thirty minutes into the trip, they realize, "it is taking too long." In their mind, they are saying: "We should be there by now." The adult understand the trip will take 40 hours. They are prepared for the time it will take for the journey. They know that there will be many stops for food, gas, bathroom breaks, stretching, and temporary lodging.

Now, ask yourself: "Which am I when it comes to my career and personal goals? The kid or the adult?"

What sets apart the two is that the adult has a sense of how long it should take to get from one point to the other. They have done the calculations and have built a plan to enjoy, or at least not be frustrated about the long trip or journey ahead. Not so much with a child.

The adult knows the variables that they may encounter along the way. It doesn't mean that they will, but they are ready, just in case. They may take into account the terrain that they will travel over. They will take into account the changes of moving from one time zone to the next, one weather cycle into the next. They will also account for how much gas they will need to use before stopping, or how many times they need to charge their e-vehicle. These and so many more are considered in the destination plan. For the kid, all they know is that I am sitting in this back seat and it looks all the same to me; and I am tired.

When you take the position of not driving your life and not doing the due diligence for the journey, things often look the same and you are at the mercy of what life is throwing at you. The perspective is different for the person who is driving their life. They are constantly making decisions and keeping their head on a swivel.

Think about this along with all of the other preparation before a person would leave for a road trip. There is the "in the moment" decisions that will happen all the way to the destinations such as four way stops, animals crossing the street abruptly, other motor vehicles not paying attention, having to drive defensively, construction, and on and on.

In our personal goals, do we believe that we can enter a new industry today and be good today or tomorrow? Do we feel we can make unrealistic jumps in our financial income? Do we believe we can build followship in a matter of days without having the skills to lead? Those who believe the answer is yes are like the children in the back seat. They do not have a mature way of thinking. Let me be one of the first to level set with you and bring you back to earth. It doesn't work that way.

Prepare for what you can control. Most people overestimate what they can do in a year and underestimate what they can do in five or ten years. This journey will take some time. Pack accordingly. Do your research on what it may look like in the days, weeks, or years ahead so that you are not disillusioned by the things you will encounter along the way. Know there will be many things to encounter, but with the right preparation, you will be able to move through this life in better spirits than those who have no awareness of what may or could happen along the way.

# Notes

# GPS: Tracking Your Progress

**W**e have to build a plan and put in mile markers to keep our motivation high. In goal-setting we call this tracking. Tracking is a method used to show us how far we have come or how much we have accomplished in reference to the goal. So if you know where you are, because you have used the "map" of life, then your plan will give you an overall reference point for timing and distance. Now, all you have to do is create a few tracking elements along the way to make sure that you are on coarse.

An example of getting twice as good in half the time is thinking of things this way. You may be going across country in a car now. It might be a nice car. But no matter how nice the car is, it will never travel at the same speed as an airplane. Most cars will only have a max speed of 150-175 mi/hr on their speedometer. On average, a plane travels 470-525 mi/hr. So in life, you may have to switch vehicles in order to reach the same location in less time.

Either vehicle will need to have some kind of GPS or tracking apparatus. When you drive a car, you have applications that can show you where you are and how far you are away from your destination. The same with flying in a plane. These days, the airlines do a good job of having in-flight Wi-Fi to keep you entertained. Along with that amenity, they will have a tracking mechanism set up to show you how far away you are from their destination.

So what does all this travel imagery have to do with getting good? Well, if you want to be great at your job, in your industry, or in the world, you have to put these things in place in your life. You have to employ a system or even an infrastructure that will remind you if you are on course to your goals or may be veering off a little.

A GPS in your life could be a coach or a mentor. It could be an accountability partner or group. Either way, you want to have someone or something set up so that you are aware of where you are in your journey. You don't want to be surprised and find out you were going the wrong way for months, years, and God forbid even decades. As wild as this may sound, more people than not, end their lives looking back and realizing they never had a GPS in their lives, and they were driven by life instead of driving their life on purpose.

# Notes

_____

_____

_____

_____

_____

_____

_____

_____

_____

_____

_____

_____

_____

_____

_____

_____

# Staying Online

In our continued parallel of navigation to our lives, understand that it is vitally important to stay online. I do not mean social media or having the best Wi-Fi available. I mean staying connected to the best sources of indicators you can have in your life. Staying online means that you are getting all of the signals needed to continue to make the best decisions for your life. Remember the journey is long and, for most of us, we have not been there before, so we will need some help along the way. You will need all the assistance afforded as you travel.

If we are going to be twice as good in half the time, we will use some methods and techniques that are not known to our friends, associates or our immediate family. Do not take offense to this. This is simply tapping into the Online GPS.

I once took my mother to Los Angeles, California. It was her first time in the city and state. I got a rental car from the airport and we were off to see the city. One of the first places I wanted to go was the world famous Rosco's Chicken and Waffles.

When we got into the car, my mother was giving me a hesitant look. I saw it but did not immediately address it. After a minute of me getting my barrens together and finding the location of the nearest Rosco's, I was ready to put the car in reverse and head over to the location for some good brunch. My mother couldn't hold it anymore.

"Do you know where you are going?" she asked.

I smiled at her and told her with all of the confidence in the world: "No, No I don't."

That definitely unnerved her.

"How are we going to get around this city if you don't know where you are going?"

I raised my cell phone and pointed to it with the other hand and said, "She, the nice lady voice on the phone, will take us anywhere we need to go in this city. So really, all I have to do is follow the directions that she gives me and make sure we always have a signal, and we are good."

I could see that seeing was believing for my mom, but nevertheless, I had used this apparatus before and knew the power of being connected to the online signal. Not only could this device get me anywhere in the city, but it could also identify if their were accidents, road closures, better routes, etc to the location.

So how do you stay online in life? Good question! Your attitude and internal beliefs keep you online. Who you are plugged up to will be a determinant for how long you will stay online. Many people who will read this will have a spiritual belief or faith in God or some higher power. If your faith is strong, then you will be confident that the right people, resources, and connections will be brought into your life to provide the assistance you need to get you to where you want to go in the right amount of time.

Some people in your life will teach you how to better manage your time so that you are 2x, 3x, or 4x as efficient as you used to be. (Remember earlier, you are only comparing yourself to yourself.) Some people will show you how to identify opportunities that will increase your financial status so that you can move closer to those goals. Others will show you how to develop as a leader of yourself and others. It really doesn't matter what you need, being connected Online, will make sure that you get exactly what you need when you need it.

Think of it this way, there are some messages that come up on your GPS, that were not planned on your journey, but because in real-time, things changed either in your favor or for your detriment, the GPS detects it and re-routes you accordingly so that you can move seamlessly toward your goal, your dream, your destiny.

The only responsibilities you have in staying online is keeping your connection charged and following the directions that are given to you. I say this with so much simplicity, but I know that it is not as easy as it sounds. Nevertheless, do what is being given to you and enjoy the journey through life, if not, many frustrations and disappoints are ahead.

How do I keep my connection charged? Meditation and prayer have been a major part of many successful people I have met and studied. Having a strong spiritual center and knowing that the Almighty is connected to everyone is what you can rest in. Why can you rest in this? If you need a sales person for your job opening and a person who is looking to pursue a career in sales is out there, the Almighty will have coordinates for both you and the person that you have never met in your life. Just like the navigation system knows what's around the corner so does the Almighty and He will not allow you to be without.

Finally, the last responsibility is following the directions. The late great Bob Proctor said it this way. When he met his mentor, Earl Nightingale, he said Mr. Nightingale told him "look at where your way has gotten you to date. If you like what you see in my life, you might want to do it my way." Like any smart person who is looking to better themselves, Bob followed the directions from Mr. Nightingale and success became his many times over.

Be open to directions from people who have a proven track record of doing the things that you want to do and being the person you would like to become. Allow success to be yours many times over in half the time.

Do You Need Help Gaining Momentum in Your Career?
Visit us at:

# MomentumLeadershipUniversity.com